THE
CROWN
AND THE SCARS

A Journey To Healing.....

NOWA ARKTRESHIA FLUDD

Copyright © 2025 by **Nowa Arktreshia Fludd**

All rights reserved. This book or any portion thereof may not be reproduced or used in any manner whatsoever without the express written permission of the publisher except for the use of brief quotations in a book review.

Printed in the United States of America

First Edition, 2025

PAPERBACK ISBN: 979-8-3492-8229-4

EBOOK ISBN: 979-8-3492-8230-0

Red Pen Edits and Consulting, LLC

www.redpeneditsllc.com

TABLE OF CONTENTS

FOREWORD 1

PREFACE 7

CHAPTER 1
The Weight of Difference 9

CHAPTER 2
A Cycle of Chaos 13

CHAPTER 3
A New Beginning in the System 17

CHAPTER 4
Finding My Place in the Chaos 19

CHAPTER 5
A New Home, A New Challenge 21

CHAPTER 6
A New Placement, A New Game 25

CHAPTER 7
Running The Show At Dream House 29

CHAPTER 8
Shattered Innocence 33

CHAPTER 9
The Weight Of Silence 35

CHAPTER 10
Fueled By Anger 39

CHAPTER 11
A Return To Familiarity 41

CHAPTER 12
A New Chapter In The Dark 45

CHAPTER 13
The Crossroads 49

CHAPTER 14
The Weight Of Love And Sacrifice 53

CHAPTER 15
Emancipation And Awakening 57

CHAPTER 16
Emancipation And Unexpected Twists 61

CHAPTER 17
Chaos, Courage, And New Beginnings 65

CHAPTER 18
A Village Of Miracles 69

CHAPTER 19
Trials, Triumphs, And Unseen Battles 73

CHAPTER 20
The Comedy Of Errors 77

CHAPTER 21
The Journey Of Healing And Redemption 81

ABOUT THE AUTHOR 85

FOREWORD

"Scars are the birth mark of an individual that has navigated the worst parts of the bowels of Hell….but made it through."

— R.L. WILSON

There are stories that entertain, stories that inform, and then there are stories that transform. **The Crown and the Scars: A Journey To Healing** is one of those rare works that does all three. In these pages, **Nowa Arktreshia Fludd**, whom I've literally known over half my life, invites us into a deeply personal and unflinchingly raw odyssey—one that navigates through the storms of abandonment, trauma, and survival, yet emerges with an unwavering declaration of resilience and redemption.

To read this book is to witness the journey of a soul determined to reclaim its power. From the weight of childhood loss to the chaos of a system that often fails those it was meant to protect, Nowa does not merely recount her past—she confronts it with a fearless honesty that demands attention. Moreover, her words do not ask for pity; they compel understanding. She does not just share struggles; she unearths the depths of what it means to fight for oneself when the world seems determined to break you.

Buried deep within the power in the ink of her pen, therein lies a prevailing theme — hope. Not the fleeting, surface-level kind, but a hope that is battle-tested, one that has been forged through betrayal, self-discovery, the bowels of Hell and the unrelenting pursuit of healing.

This is a story that does not merely say, You can survive. It declares, You can thrive. It is a resounding affirmation that no matter how deep the wounds, no matter how heavy the burdens, there is always the possibility of rising again…rising to believe, to become and to belong.

Nowa's journey is not just her own; it is one that mirrors the silent battles of many. There are those who will read these pages and see themselves in her struggles, in the moments of loneliness, in the cycles of chaos, in the weight of silence that too often accompanies trauma.

Additionally, they will also see themselves in her victories—in the courage to break free, in the strength to stand tall despite the scars, and in the power to rewrite the narrative that life once tried to dictate for her.

What makes The Crown and the Scars extraordinary is its unfiltered authenticity. There is absolutely NO attempt to soften the blows or romanticize the hardships…at all. Instead, Nowa tells her truth in its rawest form, ensuring that every emotion, every hardship, and every triumph is felt as deeply as it was lived. Her willingness to be vulnerable, to expose the most painful corners of her past, is not only courageous but transformative for those who have never found the words to articulate their own suffering. In one passage, she recalls a pivotal moment from her childhood:

"I walked into my room to find all my belongings packed, my heart racing as I overheard the harsh words that pierced through the air:

'I'd never get another nasty hog like you if I were on my deathbed.' Those words are etched in my memory; they were a cruel reminder of my worthlessness in someone else's eyes. In that moment, I stood frozen, speechless. You don't talk back to adults, especially when they are filled with anger and disdain."

How many have stood in that same silence, carrying the unbearable weight of words meant to diminish them? How many have questioned their own value because someone else failed to see it? And yet, Nowa stands today, not as a victim of those words, but as a victor over them. Her story is proof that pain does not have the final say; in fact, she has chosen to make pain pay…to monetize her misery, and to, instead of living a life of affliction, live a life of impact.

There is a rare kind of strength in allowing the world to see your scars. Society often teaches us to hide them, to present ourselves as whole even when we are shattered inside. Nowa does the opposite—she does not shy away from her wounds but instead displays them as evidence of her survival, as proof that brokenness does not mean ruin.

Every page of this book is a testament to that truth. She takes us through the darkest corridors of her past, yet she does so with an undeniable light—a spirit that refuses to be dimmed…a force to be reckoned with.

What lies ahead in these pages is not just a memoir, but a movement of truth-telling. It is a work that speaks to the wounded and the weary, to the ones who have been knocked down by life but refuse to stay there. It is a declaration that our past, no matter how painful, does not define us. Rather, it refines us. Selah

It carves out resilience where there was once despair, cultivates strength where there was once fear, and shapes us into versions of ourselves we never imagined we could become.

This book is for the ones still fighting, for the ones who have ever questioned their worth, for those who have been told they are not enough. It is for the ones who have been bruised by life but refuse to be broken. It is for the ones who need to be reminded that scars do not signify defeat—they signify survival. And in that survival, there is a crown waiting.

May the words within these pages find those who need them most. May they stir something deep in the soul of every reader—a conviction that they, too, can rise from the ashes. And may Nowa's journey remind us all that no matter what we have endured, we are still standing. We are still here. And that alone is worth celebrating.

Finally, as an author, I'm personally aware that a foreword is simply an introduction to a book — it is comprised of highlights about the book itself or even characteristics about the author. However, I'd like to close this treatise by sharing something to the author:

Dear Nowa,

Through your journey, you have given others permission to own their own. You have laid bare your truth, and in doing so, you have illuminated a path for others to follow. Your story is not just a personal testimony—it is a lifeline to those who feel unseen, unheard, and unworthy of healing. This book will be a light to many who are still navigating their own darkness, a testament that healing is not just possible but inevitable for those who dare to embrace it.

Bishop-Elect Ra'Shan L. Wilson

PREFACE

Every story begins somewhere. My story starts in the shadows of pain and adversity, where I learned that life is often a paradox—a blend of joy and sorrow, hope and despair. As I pen these words, I reflect on the myriad of experiences that have shaped me into the woman I am today. This memoir is a journey through the tumultuous landscape of my life, a testament to the resilience that lies within us all.

When I look back at my childhood, I see a canvas painted with both vibrant colors and dark hues. Each brushstroke represents a moment of triumph or tragedy, from the innocence of my early years to the complexities of adolescence and adulthood. I have navigated through a series of challenges—sexual assault, homelessness, and the turbulent waters of foster care—each leaving an indelible mark on my soul.

Yet, it is not just the struggles that define me; it is how I have chosen to rise above them. In the face of overwhelming odds, I discovered the strength that comes from vulnerability and the power of faith. My journey is a story of survival, but it is also one of hope and transformation. It is a reminder that even in our darkest moments, we can find light and purpose.

The title of this memoir, "The Crown and the Scars," reflects the duality of my existence. The crown symbolizes the dignity and strength I have cultivated through my trials, while the scars are the tangible reminders of battles fought and won. Together, they tell a story of resilience, one that I believe resonates with many who have faced their own challenges.

As you delve into these pages, I invite you to walk alongside me. This is not just my story; it is a collective narrative that echoes the experiences of countless individuals who have faced adversity. My hope is that by sharing my journey, I can inspire others to embrace their scars and recognize the crowns they wear—crowns of strength, determination, and faith.

Thank you for joining me on this journey. May you find courage in your own stories and the unwavering belief that, like me, you can overcome.

CHAPTER 1

The Weight of Difference

Some of my earliest memories are tinged with a profound sense of difference. I recall the moment I first learned that I was adopted, a term that floated around me like a foreign language I couldn't quite grasp. "We adopted her at eight months," I heard someone say during an introduction, and in that instant, my heart sank. Wait! I'm not yours? A wave of confusion and fear washed over me. Who is mine?

I don't know much about my birth. All I know is that my biological mother said I was born with a "halo" over my head. I believe her! I was told she took pride in being my mother and was absolutely proud to have a daughter. Unfortunately, I didn't discover this until I was 44 years old. I often wonder how different my life might have been if I had known she wanted me from the very beginning. But on the flip side, if I had known, you wouldn't be getting to know me right now. So, a win is a win!

My mother allegedly met my donor when his ship docked in Charleston, SC, during his service in the Navy. She got pregnant, had me, but also battled an addiction that ultimately had her in its grip. At that time, I had one older brother, but I'm unsure of his story during those early years. All I know is that at just eight months old, I was found sitting outside in a dirty diaper,… alone, … with no adults around. I was rescued. This was the beginning of a journey fraught with challenges.

Growing up, my family structure felt like a puzzle with missing pieces. While I found comfort in the familiarity of my surroundings, I often felt a disconnection, a feeling that I didn't quite belong. However, for the sake of clarity in this narrative, I won't delve into those complexities. Instead, I'll focus on the shadows that began to creep into my childhood.

My first encounter with trauma came in an unexpected and horrific form. My nephew moved in with us, struggling with behavioral issues that would soon turn our home into a battleground of fear and confusion. It was during this time that I was forced into a nightmare I couldn't escape. He made me perform oral sex on him, wielding threats that tightened around my young heart: if I told anyone, my parents would die. The weight of that threat was suffocating. I loved my parents, and the thought of losing them paralyzed me with fear. So, I did as he said, unaware of the gravity of what was happening. Afterward, I felt hollow, burdened with shame and sadness, grappling with an experience I couldn't understand.

At just eight years old, I reached a breaking point. My first suicide attempt came in a moment of desperate hopelessness. I swallowed an entire bottle of Bayer Aspirin, believing that this was my escape, my way out of a world that felt unbearably heavy. I lay down, surrendering to the darkness, only to awaken in a panic, realizing I had lost my hearing. For days, I could only read lips, a surreal and isolating experience. Can you imagine the disappointment of waking up, believing you had found freedom, only to face the reality of your life again? My little heart shattered further as I continued to endure the abuse, feeling like a failure for not succeeding in my escape.

With no one to confide in, I turned to self-harm as a misguided coping mechanism. I started cutting myself, using objects around me as a release for the pain that festered inside. I struck matches, mesmerized by the flickering flames, desperately searching for a way to escape my reality. My closet became my sanctuary, a place to hide from the world, believing that if I could just retreat from the pain, it would somehow fade away. But hiding does not make the pain disappear; it only pushes it deeper, forcing me to confront hard realities that I would later grapple with throughout my life.

This chapter of my life was filled with darkness, but it laid the foundation for the resilience that would eventually emerge. As I navigate through the scars of my past, I hope to shed light on the journey of survival and healing that has brought me to where I am today.

CHAPTER 2

A Cycle of Chaos

The weight of my childhood experiences hung heavily over me as I entered the tumultuous years of adolescence. During this time, I had the opportunity to meet my biological mother and visit her home on weekends. Those visits were a mixed bag of emotions. My mother struggled with addiction, often leaving my older brother and me alone in her apartment for hours with no food. In those moments of hunger, I quickly became friends with the neighbor's kids because, well, who doesn't want to eat? My best friend in the complex, Ashley Shores, was a Caucasian girl named Tammy. She and her little sister would often invite me over to eat and play, providing a much-needed escape from my reality.

Being forced to perform a sexual act at such a young age had irrevocably changed me. It left scars that I carried into my interactions with others. I cherished the time spent with other children, even as I grappled with the trauma hidden beneath the surface. One day, during a visit to my mother's apartment, I witnessed a horrific scene. My mother would often sleep during the day and go out at night, locking us inside her room while she drifted off. I remember seeing Tammy struggling with her dad, a scene that unfolded like a nightmare before my eyes. I screamed for my mother to help, but she told me to mind my business. I watched helplessly as he stabbed her, my cries echoing in the silence of her indifference. It wasn't until a manhunt was underway that she finally stirred from her slumber.

At this point in my life, I was a cocktail of trauma—adopted, having attempted suicide, enduring molestation, and now witnessing my best friend get killed. I didn't know how to cope. In an attempt to escape the chaos, I turned to carving soap, a craft I saw on ETV. I knew I would be punished if I got caught, so I cleverly hid the knife, pillow, and soap under my bed, returning them to their rightful places when everyone was asleep.

Eventually, my nephew moved out, which meant my body was free from the burden of abuse, yet my mind remained shackled. My behavior had evidently spiraled out of control, leading to my placement with my grandmother—my biological mother's mother. I thought this change might bring a sense of fun and stability, but I was sorely mistaken.

I no longer had my coping mechanisms at my disposal. I had to change schools and adjust to living with my grandmother and her husband, a man I had never met. This transition added another layer of abandonment to my already heavy load. My biological mother had given me away, and now here I was, with a stranger. I was around nine years old, a mere child grappling with the aftermath of my traumatic past.

As for my biological mother? You won't hear much of her in this chapter, but for context, she was serving a 15-year sentence for beating my grandmother's husband. My family had its share of struggles with alcohol, and my grandmother was no exception. When she drank, her husband would beat her to a bloody pulp. I was only nine, yet I found myself enveloped in a cycle of domestic violence that left me terrified.

One day, after one of those brutal beatings, my grandmother signed me out of school and took me back to my adoptive parents. She confessed that she wasn't strong enough to protect me from him and warned me never to mention that she brought me back. I remember being left there with no food or water, sitting outside until it was dark, waiting for my parents to return. When they finally did, I was taken back to my grandmother's. She denied everything, and the cycle of violence continued.

But then, a glimmer of hope appeared: a law passed, and my biological mother was released early. I was thrilled to meet her again after a two-year separation. That night, I went to bed feeling safe—until I was violently awakened by my grandmother's husband, bursting into my room completely naked. He jumped on top of me, forcing my legs apart. I could feel the tip of his genitalia against me, and as I screamed for my mother, my grandmother stood there, whispering for him to stop but not intervening. Fortunately, my mother arrived just in time, and he was thrown outside into the snow.

However, my mother eventually returned to prison, and not before she beat me senseless for something I didn't do—thinking I had stolen money that my grandmother had actually taken. I was left bruised and broken, officially hating her. When the police came to take her away, I felt a sense of relief.

Not long after, I fell violently ill and had to be rushed to the ER. My adoptive parents met my grandmother there, and in my filthy state, my adoptive mother took me back in. I started therapy, and for a brief moment, it felt like everything was on the mend. But that peace was short-lived. Once I moved back home, I reverted to my old coping mechanisms.

One day, I forgot to return the knife I used to carve my soap, and my adoptive mother discovered it hidden beneath my pillow. The therapist told her I was homicidal, and just like that, I was sent away again. I was just a girl trying to carve soap.

And so, the chaos continued, cranking the car of my life into uncertain territory.

CHAPTER 3
A New Beginning in the System

I remember the day I came home from school, just 11 years old, and everything changed. I walked into my room to find all of my belongings packed. My heart raced as I overheard the harsh words that pierced through the air: "I'd never get another nasty hog like you if I were on my deathbed." Those words are etched in my memory; they were a cruel reminder of my worthlessness in someone else's eyes. In that moment, I stood frozen, speechless. You don't talk back to adults, especially when they are filled with anger and disdain.

As the conversation continued, I listened helplessly as I was labeled ungrateful for not reacting to the news I was being sent away. The shock settled over me like a heavy blanket, and soon, I found myself loaded into a car, and taken to the Department of Social Services. It was the day my figurative car crashed, and I was thrust into a world I had never anticipated—one where I would become a ward of the state.

Yet, amidst the chaos, an angel entered my life. Her name was Cynthia Jenkins, my social worker, and she would stand by me for over 15 years. As we sat together in her office for what felt like hours, searching for a placement, I realized that nothing could have prepared me for the jungle I was about to navigate—this tumultuous life.

Cynthia found me an emergency shelter at the Carolina Youth Development Center. As she drove me to Lackawanna Boulevard, tears streamed down my face. I cried for the loss of my home, my family, and the sense of security I had never truly known. All she could do was reassure me with the words I was too afraid to believe: "You'll be okay."

Upon my arrival at the shelter, I underwent intake procedures, answering questions that felt invasive and overwhelming. Cynthia spoke on my behalf when I couldn't find the words. But as the process concluded, I ran to the locked front door, convinced my mother would come to get me. I clung to that hope, desperate for her presence. They allowed me to sleep on the floor by the front door, my heart racing with anticipation, but as the night wore on, it became painfully clear: she wasn't coming. Abandoned again.

This marked the beginning of my journey through the foster care system—a world filled with uncertainty, fear, and the relentless search for belonging.

CHAPTER 4

Finding My Place in the Chaos

Walking into the shelter for the first time was an overwhelming experience. The air was thick with the unmistakable stench of urine and the smell of Mop and Glo. It was a sensory overload, and I couldn't escape it. The house mom, Ms. Carolyn, was a feisty woman who cooked and cleaned like clockwork, yet the odor lingered stubbornly, a constant reminder of the reality I now faced. You eventually got used to it, but that first day was a lot to process.

Meeting the other kids was an eye-opening experience. I was trying to project a tough exterior, but I knew deep down that I was just a girl from the suburbs. To gain some respect, I found myself stretching the truth, telling little lies to fit in. Surprisingly, it worked; I never got into a single fight. That was my goal in this shelter filled with kids from different backgrounds who had seen things I could barely imagine.

A typical day in the shelter revolved around routines. Mornings began with checking the board for our daily chores, completing them by the allotted time, and participating in whatever recreational activities were planned for the day. Sometimes, we'd go to the park, other times to the movies, depending on who felt up to taking fifteen kids on an outing. We were a wild bunch, but amidst the chaos, I found friendships that meant the world to me.

Jessica Rabon became my sister. You couldn't convince her she wasn't black, and to this day, I love her fiercely. She was always there for me, ready to "knock your head off" if anyone dared to cross me. Our friendship filled a void in my heart, making me feel wanted, valued, and seen. But as I transitioned to a new school, I faced a different challenge—most of the girls hated me and wanted to fight. They loved to say I acted "cute," and I knew Jess would defend me without hesitation.

In this new environment, I realized something important: no one really knew me, so I could become whoever I wanted to be. I began adopting a new persona, embodying the persona of "Taushia." I transformed into a bougie, cute, ghetto girl who embraced her sexuality. I wore revealing, tight clothes, giving everyone a reason to hate me. I was determined to make my mark.

But after more than six months in the shelter, I received the news that would change everything. I was settling into my new life, and then came the words I dreaded: "Damn, they found you a home, Nowa. Put your stuff in garbage bags; you move tomorrow." I felt a wave of emotions wash over me. Tomorrow was my 11th birthday.

"Happy Birthday! Go pack!"

The excitement and dread crashed together in my chest. I had just begun to carve out a space for myself in this chaotic world, and now it was all changing again.

CHAPTER 5
A New Home, A New Challenge

The next morning, I woke up with a mixture of excitement and anxiety swirling inside me. It was my 11th birthday, a day that should have been filled with joy and celebration, but instead, it marked the beginning of yet another upheaval in my life. I packed my belongings into garbage bags, a stark reminder of how transient my existence felt. Each item represented a fragment of my past, and I wondered if I would ever truly belong anywhere.

As I was driven to my new home, I couldn't help but feel a sense of dread. What would this new family be like? Would they accept me? Would they understand the complexities of my history? The questions swirled in my mind as the car rolled to a stop in front of a modest house.

The family that greeted me was warm but unfamiliar. They were kind and eager to welcome me, but I couldn't shake the feeling of being an outsider. They had their own routines, their own traditions, and here I was, a stranger stepping into their world. I was acutely aware of my differences, and I felt the weight of my past pressing down on me.

Initially, I tried to fit in, to be the "good" girl they wanted. I wanted to show them that I could be worthy of their love and acceptance. But the baggage I carried was heavy, and I struggled to shake off the emotional scars from my childhood. I often found myself retreating into my shell, grappling with feelings of inadequacy and fear of rejection.

School was another hurdle. I had to adjust to a new environment, a new set of peers, and the ongoing challenge of proving myself. The girls from my previous school had already set the tone for how I was perceived, and I worried that the same challenges would follow me into this new chapter. I felt the need to put on a façade, to once again become Taushia—the confident, bold girl who wasn't afraid to stand out.

But the reality was, I was still just a scared little girl inside. I missed my friends from the shelter, particularly Jessica, who had become my sister by choice. I longed for the comfort of our bond, the reassurance that someone understood my struggles. I sent her text messages, hoping to maintain our connection despite the distance.

As I settled into my new routine, I began to uncover more about the family I had joined. They had their own struggles, their own stories, and I realized that everyone carries their own burdens. I started to find solace in their kindness, in the little moments we shared—family dinners, game nights, and even the mundane routines of life. Slowly, I allowed myself to trust them, to let down the walls I had built around my heart.

But my past wasn't done haunting me yet. Memories of my time in the shelter and the trauma I had endured bubbled to the surface, often at the most unexpected times. I struggled with nightmares and flashbacks that left me shaken and anxious. I didn't want to burden my new family with my pain, so I kept it all bottled up inside.

CHAPTER 6
A New Placement, A New Game

I won't linger too long on this next placement, as some things transpired that I still refuse to touch! They know, though. They know! What I can share is that I found myself in trouble at this new home—a place that felt like another maze in my already complicated life—because I simply wouldn't keep my space clean. Child, I didn't even know how! At 11 years old, I had never been made to manage my own space, so the concept of tidying up was as foreign to me as living on Mars.

One fateful day, I returned home from school with my backpack slung over my shoulder, only to be met with the sight of my belongings packed up in garbage bags, ready for departure. "Back to Carolina Youth Development Center (CYDC) I go!", I thought. A surprising rush of happiness washed over me. It felt like returning to familiar territory, a place where I had begun to carve out a semblance of comfort. But that joy was short-lived, like a bubble bursting in the wind.

When I arrived back at CYDC, my heart sank as I learned that Jessica, my sister in spirit and my unwavering source of strength, was gone. She had been placed in a different home, leaving an emptiness where our bond had flourished. My journey in the shelter had been brief, but it had mattered, and now I felt that familiar weight of loneliness settle in.

Not long after, I was offered a spot in a high-management group home just a stone's throw away from the shelter. It was a co-ed facility, housing about ten kids at a time, between the ages of 12 and 15. As I crossed the yard with my bags, I felt a mix of apprehension and anticipation. This was yet another chapter in my life, and I was determined to make the most of it.

Upon stepping into the group home, I immediately began to scan my new surroundings, eyes darting from one corner to the other. The walls were painted in muted colors, and the air was filled with the scent of cleaning supplies—a stark contrast to the chaos of my previous experiences. I quickly assessed the staff, looking for the weak spots among them—those who were easy to manipulate—and I went in for the successful kill. After all, who goes to prison and doesn't learn a few tricks along the way? That's exactly what I did.

I moved in and started running the show, baby. I quickly found my voice in this new environment, asserting myself among the other kids and establishing my place. The energy in the dorm was palpable: a mixture of laughter, tension, and the occasional burst of rebellion from kids trying to carve out their identities in a world that had often cast them aside.

I learned how to navigate the system, to play the game, and to keep myself safe. I would strategically charm the staff when needed, and when they weren't looking, I'd orchestrate my own little operations among the other kids. We formed alliances, shared secrets, and plotted minor rebellions against the rules that felt stifling. The group home became a stage where I could demonstrate my resilience and adaptability - a place where I could be whoever I wanted to be.

Each day was a new adventure, filled with the unexpected twists and turns of life in a facility. We'd gather in the common area for group activities, where I'd showcase my newfound persona, laughing and joking with the other kids, while secretly maintaining the distance that kept my heart safe. The friendships I formed were like fragile glass—beautiful but easily shattered. Yet, I embraced the chaos, knowing that this was my life and I was ready to take on whatever challenges lay ahead.

CHAPTER 7

Running The Show At Dream House

At the "Dream House," I quickly established myself as a force to be reckoned with. My charm and quick wit made me a favorite among the staff, to the point where they affectionately dubbed me "junior staff." Can you believe it? Here I was, an 11-year-old girl, trusted with the keys to the kingdom! In a high-management group home like this, every door was locked 24 hours a day, but that didn't deter me. Oh no, I had my own ways of breaching those barriers.

I realized at a young age that being charming was a powerful tool. With a smile and a clever quip, I could turn the tide in my favor. The staff didn't just see me as another kid in the system; they saw me as someone who could handle responsibility. And I was more than willing to use that to my advantage.

One day, I came home from school with my backpack slung over one shoulder and a spring in my step. The atmosphere buzzed with the familiar energy of the house, a mix of laughter and the distant sounds of kids being kids. We had our ways of knowing who was working that day, usually based on the cars parked outside. That afternoon, I spotted a sleek black Honda Accord—definitely not one of the usual vehicles.

As I strutted through the front door, I channeled my inner diva, big-dogging my way into the living room. "Who working that we don't know?" I called out, my voice echoing with a confidence that belied my age.

Out of the office emerged a tall, skinny, light-skinned lady with an air of authority. She had a serious demeanor, and I could tell right away she meant business. "You must be Taushia," she said, eyeing me with a mix of curiosity and apprehension.

I squinted at her, sizing her up. "You are?" I shot back, not one to shy away from a little banter.

"I'm Tonya Houston, your new house mother," she replied, her tone firm but not unkind. "You can head to your room and wait for instructions."

I paused for a moment, taking in her presence. There was something about her that rubbed me the wrong way, but I played it cool. "When I get home from school, I get apple juice. It keeps me calm," I said with a mischievous grin creeping across my face. That was a bold-faced lie; I just adored apple juice with a passion.

Tonya's brows furrowed in response. "Not today. Go to your room," she commanded.

And just like that, I felt the spark of rebellion ignite within me. That was the day I started plotting to make her life a living hell. I could already see it: the little pranks, the playful disruptions, the strategic chaos. I was determined to test the limits of her patience, to see just how far I could push her before she cracked.

In the days that followed, I began my campaign of mischief. I'd sneak into the pantry and swipe snacks, leaving little clues to confuse the staff. I'd orchestrate elaborate schemes with the other kids, setting up harmless traps that would send Tonya on a wild goose chase. I was like a little general, rallying my troops to join in on the fun, all while maintaining my façade of innocence.

Tonya, for her part, tried to maintain control. She'd call us in for meetings, laying down the law with her no-nonsense attitude. But I could see the frustration flicker in her eyes as she struggled to rein in the chaos. Each time she tried to assert her authority, I'd counter with a quick comeback or a playful retort, and soon enough, she became just another player in my game.

But beneath all the antics and the laughter, there were moments of vulnerability. I was still that scared little girl trying to navigate a tumultuous world. The pranks were a way to cope, a distraction from the deeper emotions that lurked beneath the surface. In my heart, I craved stability and acceptance, and I was determined to carve out a place for myself in this new home.

As the weeks rolled on, I began to realize that Tonya wasn't just an obstacle to overcome; she was a person in her own right. If I could learn to navigate her quirks and frustrations, perhaps I could forge a bond that went beyond the playful banter. Maybe, just maybe, I could find a way to coexist with her—while still running the show, of course.

And so, the stage was set for a battle of wills, where laughter and mischief mingled with the complexities of growing up in a world that often felt unfair. I was ready to embrace whatever came next, knowing that I had the charm and resilience to face it all head-on.

CHAPTER 8

Shattered Innocence

So, I thought I was living my best life at Dream House until Tonya showed up to break up my hoochie mama ways! Can you believe this lady made me throw away any ripped jeans or shorts and any revealing tops? I mean, she didn't know that my "titties" liked to be out! How dare she! I was mad, for real!

We barely got clothes to begin with, and here she was, tossing them away like they were old rags. Tonya had me wearing a sweatsuit—sweatshirt and sweatpants—for months, trying to prove a point that my body was a temple. What did my 12-year-old self care about that? I felt hot and fast, and I wanted to express that! Little did I know, Tonya was about to change my life in ways I didn't even understand at the time.

Tonya was actually the one who introduced me to the first church I ever became a member of: the Abundant Life Tabernacle AME Zion Church. Yeah, you didn't know I was a church girl, huh? I grew up Pentecostal Holiness, baby! I'm a proud church girl, and I owe a lot of that to Tonya. She set me on a path that I would need to reflect back on in my adult years, whether I liked it or not.

Now, let's discuss Debbie Dawson, or "Debbo," as I affectionately called her. She was one of the group home staff members who absolutely had me ROTTEN! While Tonya was enforcing the dress code, Debbo was letting me do what I wanted, when I wanted. Don't tell Tonya! I loved them both immensely to this day. My life at Dream House felt magical, a whirlwind of love and chaos, laughter and tears.

Take a fleeting moment to consider why it felt so magical. I had the opportunity to do some amazing adventurous things that I had only dreamed of before: white water rafting, kayaking, skiing. It was the best three years of my life—until it wasn't.

You see, I had a best friend in high school named Sasha. She had a brother named Debo, and I'd go to their house after school frequently since we walked home together daily. Now, Debo and I had a little private something going on, even though he had a girlfriend. I found myself, for the first time, engaging in sex to keep a man's attention. Those were the ages I discovered the art of seduction and persuasion! I thought I had him wrapped around my finger—until he took it.

Yep, you read that right. He held me down and took it, even when I said no. I walked home that day crying, bleeding, and utterly alone. That day changed me! I knew from that moment forward that I'd get them—men—before they ever got me again. I felt like a part of me died that day. Ashes to ashes.

CHAPTER 9

The Weight Of Silence

No, I didn't tell anyone. Sexual stuff made me think that someone would die if I spoke up. Plus, he was a star basketball player; I didn't want anyone mad at me. So, I suffered silently. Sasha's house wouldn't see me again, and just as I was getting nestled into this new house mother, I faced another traumatic event—I was raped, and I had no way to cope. It was pretty bad.

Then, the most affectionate and loving female moved in. She had a rough-and-tumble spirit, complete with her Afro puffs, and we hit it off instantly. Connica (KUH-KNEE-SHUH) Perry! We were as thick as thieves. And if you're wondering, yes, we still communicate here and there, 33 years later. Yep, you read that right! Are you even 33 yet? LOL! But no, she was 10 toes down for me.

Connica had the one thing I longed for: family. Her family would send her a box of clothes and sneakers every month. They'd send money for her to get her hair braided, etc. Me? Nope. No one called, no one came to see me, and no one said, "Let's get her a pair of draws." Nothing. I had no one but her. So, she shared her family with me, but mostly, she shared her FINE hazel-eyed brother, Craig! Babyyyyyyyy, I loved me some CRAIG! You hear me? We'd talk on the phone all the time while she had weekend visits with their mom. He would come down with them, but it would be me and him, hugged up under a tree or walking the campus as his sister enjoyed time with their mom.

Now, you should start seeing the repetitive cycles. What do you think happened not too long after? You got it—Connica was returned back home. And once again, I was alone.

Now, let me set the record straight because I can't let me and my girl go out like this. Just because I haven't mentioned everything in this chapter doesn't mean you should think we were absolute angels. Connica and I were modern-day Frick and Frack. If she got in trouble, I got in trouble.

We had this small room in our group home called "timeout," an 8 x 8 cell where you were placed alone for acting out. The door had locks on the outside, so you couldn't get out. It was a literal punishment cell. I spent a lot of time locked up, lol. I started house riots. I organized group runway nights where we'd all jump out of our windows and run away, forcing staff to call the police to come find us. I was an absolute terror. I frequently ran away and defied anyone who told me what to do because, in my mind, I was this new person I had created. I built a wall around my heart, and I dared anyone to approach me or say anything wrong. I was ready to pop off.

Let's step back for a moment.

Remember when I told you that Connica left to go back with her mom? Good! Well, not only was I losing a sister, but I was losing my man, and that sent me into a tailspin. I was so depressed. I wasn't going to school, and some days I wouldn't eat. Staff couldn't figure out what was wrong with me because I wouldn't share it. I was lonely and down. I just couldn't understand why people kept getting taken away from me.

But I knew a bittersweet moment was coming up—my 15th birthday. Now, you might ask why that mattered. Yes, I had been at Dream House for four years, but you couldn't stay in that home once you turned 15. Everyone fought for me to try and keep me there, even though I was outside of the age range, but they just wouldn't approve it.

So here we go on another journey. You ready?

CHAPTER 10
Fueled By Anger

At this stage in my life, I had come to the painful resolve that I was worthless and that no one stayed in my life. I became insufferable. People couldn't even look at me without fearing I'd start a fight. There wasn't just one thing that triggered me—are you human? Triggered! LOL.

One day, I was in the hallways, riding high on my popularity with the fellas but not so much with the ladies. I found out that a girl and I were dating the same boy, and it didn't sit well with her. One day, as he and I spoke in the halls, she squared me up. I ignored her and kept laughing at whatever non-funny thing he said.

When the bell rang for lunch, wearing your man's coat was a badge of honor. I strutted into the courtyard, rocking his leather coat, feeling on top of the world. Suddenly, I heard her voice cut through the noise.

"Is that Gerald's jacket?"

I replied, "Yeah," and before I knew it, we were in a fierce fight.

It was brutal. I suddenly felt two sharp bites in my chest, near my heart. Confused and in pain, I looked down to see what was biting me. To my horror, I realized it was an ice pick embedded in my chest. In that moment, both of us had gaping holes in our bodies, remnants of a fight that spiraled out of control.

Needless to say, I got expelled. By the time I arrived back at the group home, DSS had my things packed. They shipped me four hours away to Greenville, SC, where I would spend the next year. I arrived there on May 7, 1995, and moved back home on May 7, 1996.

In Greenville, I was placed in an independent living group home that was supposed to teach me life skills. Child, please! At 15-16, it was an awkward year, and I won't dwell too much on that!

When I finally returned to Charleston, I was 16 but looked 20, and I was ready to mingle. LOL!

CHAPTER 11

A Return To Familiarity

When I got back to Charleston, I was buzzing with excitement. If you haven't figured it out yet, I was returning to my favorite place—CYDC. You remember, the place I had just left a year prior. I could hardly contain my joy as I stepped through those familiar doors. The atmosphere was filled with a sense of belonging, and there were a lot of familiar faces eager to see me again. Many of them needed my help, and I was more than willing to provide it. I was junior staff, remember? LOL. It felt good to be in a position where I could support others, even if I was still figuring out my own life.

The biggest challenge ahead would be finding a permanent place to call home. Despite the uncertainty looming over me, I wasn't focusing on that; I just knew to savor these fleeting moments. Each laugh, every shared memory, and the comfort of familiar surroundings brought a sense of warmth I had longed for during my time away.

However, my time back at the emergency shelter was short-lived. On the same campus, there was an independent living program I got accepted into, and I was ready for a new adventure. With my trash bags in tow, I dragged them across the street, feeling a mix of anticipation and nostalgia. I was hopeful about this new chapter and ready to embrace whatever came next.

Once I settled into the independent living program, reality hit me like a freight train. I quickly realized that this was going to be a problem. They had rules—with consequences. What was that? LOL. The rules felt suffocating; I had grown accustomed to a life of defiance. Breaking the rules became a badge of honor for me, a way to assert my independence. But there was a fine line between independence and rebellion, and I often found myself crossing it.

Yet my experience in this particular group home wasn't solely about the rules or my defiance. It was about who I met while I was there—Cynthia Gathers! My house mother! A feisty, spirited woman from New York, Cynthia played no games. She had a way of commanding attention and respect, and I found myself drawn to her immediately. Do you want to know why she's important? Glad you asked!

Cynthia was the person who told me that God called me and that I needed to heed to His word. She made God real to me in ways I never experienced before. Through her guidance, I began to confront the struggles I had carried since I was that 8-year-old girl, lost and confused. Cynthia became a beacon of hope, someone who saw potential in me when I couldn't see it in myself.

Our conversations were a lifeline. She would often share her wisdom, reminding me that I was worthy of love and purpose. She had a unique ability to connect with me on a spiritual level, helping me navigate the stormy waters of my emotions. I remember one afternoon, sitting on the porch, tears streaming down my face as I shared my fears and doubts. Cynthia held my hands and prayed with me, and in that moment, I felt a flicker of hope ignite within me.

Unfortunately, my rebellious spirit eventually led to me getting kicked out of that home. It wasn't long before my defiance caught up with me, and I lost touch with Cynthia. I felt the weight of that loss, as if a part of my support system had been ripped away. But fate had a plan; I was able to see her again over 20 years later, just a year before she passed away. We managed to get a photo together, and this book is dedicated to her memory. It was only right. How else can I say thank you for rescuing me?

After being kicked out of the group home for my defiance, I was sent to a foster home that I would describe as one of the entrances to hell. It was a stark contrast to the warmth and structure I had experienced at CYDC. The environment was chaotic and filled with uncertainty, and I quickly realized that I was in over my head.

"What have you gotten yourself into, Taushia?" I asked myself repeatedly as I faced the harsh realities of this new living situation. The atmosphere was tense, and the rules were even more rigid than before. I felt lost, like a ship adrift at sea without a compass. The challenges were overwhelming, and I struggled to find my footing.

As I navigated this new chapter, I couldn't help but reflect on the lessons I learned from Cynthia. Her words echoed in my mind: "You are worthy, Taushia." I clung to those words as I faced the unknown, hoping to find a way to reclaim my identity and purpose.

CHAPTER 12
A New Chapter In The Dark

So, here I am in this new foster home, led to a room that was basically a storage space with a bed crammed inside. The moment I stepped into that room, disbelief washed over me. I couldn't believe my social worker was leaving me here. The environment felt oppressive and bleak, and a sense of dread gripped my heart. I felt as though I had been cast aside, like an unwanted item shoved into the back of a closet.

That evening, I was called in for dinner. As I sat at the table, I was handed a list of rules that felt more like a prison sentence than guidelines for living. It was at that moment that I noticed the chains on the cabinets and refrigerator. I was floored. Why did this lady have her food locked up? It was a surreal reality check that made my stomach churn.

But what truly shattered my sense of safety was when I returned to my room and discovered a padlock on the outside of my door. Every night, I was locked in, forced to find makeshift solutions for basic needs. Can you imagine? I had to find things to urinate in at night because I couldn't get a cup or anything—the cabinets were locked. The humiliation was unbearable. I was reduced to sneaking food to school so I could hide it in my backpack, along with a cup I kept for emergencies.

As the days turned into weeks, the oppressive atmosphere weighed heavily on me. The isolation was suffocating. I found myself counting the hours until I could escape the confines of that room, even if it was just for a brief moment. But the reality was that I was trapped—not only physically but emotionally as well.

The situation escalated when I made a distressing confession about her husband. He had unlocked my door one night when he shouldn't have, and when I finally mustered the courage to speak out, I was taken to the hospital for a rape kit. The kit came back inconclusive (right), and instead of receiving support and understanding, I was accused of wanting it. The betrayal cut deeper than any physical wound. I was told by my foster mother that she wanted me gone. That's when I found myself homeless once again at 17.

This time, the emergency shelter was full, so I was placed in a series of emergency foster homes until they found one that could take me for a full weekend. Little did I know, that placement would turn into two years.

Writing this chapter is incredibly difficult because so much joy and pain unfolded during this time. Some names have been omitted; some for their protection, and others for mine. But let's dive in.

I arrived at this new home in the middle of the summer, and I remember it being blisteringly hot. Yet, I wore a coat—a protective barrier that made me feel closed off and safe after everything I had endured. The coat became my shield, a way to insulate myself from the harsh realities of my life. In this foster home, I reunited with

Mia, a young lady I had met in one of my previous group homes. She was one of the prettiest red girls you'd ever seen, and I was excited to see her again. To my surprise, it was actually her little sister, Robin, who was there. To this day, she is my baby sister. Robin was essential in making me feel nostalgic, reminding me of a simpler time before everything spiraled out of control.

Then there was "TeeTee." You know that comedic relief chunky girl in all the movies? That was her! I was trying to wallow in my sadness and have an attitude about being in yet another foster home, and she was having none of it. "Uh uh… come on, we're going to the laundromat!" No, for real—we went to the laundromat. As we loaded clothes into the washer, I felt a flicker of joy I hadn't experienced in a long time. I quickly learned that the laundromat became an escape from the prison I was voluntarily signing up for.

I had so much fun with Robin and TeeTee that when the weekend ended, I was asked if I wanted to stay or go. I fought with the idea of leaving but ultimately chose to stay. What I gained from this experience were two sisters for life. We formed a bond that transcended the chaos surrounding us. We laughed, cried, and navigated the complexities of our lives together - each of us bringing our unique strengths to the table.

We all had our individual struggles, but I can only share MY account. I've opted not to go into all of it because I want to keep the focus on my journey, but just know—what doesn't kill you makes you stronger. This home, especially, made TeeTee and me stronger. I'm in the process of writing a book on foster care, and I'll be more descriptive there. But yes, the three of us are still going strong.

As time passed, however, the challenges persisted. I ended up getting pregnant with my son, and one of the young ladies in the house decided to tell on me. The weight of the world felt like it was crashing down on my shoulders when I received the news that I couldn't stay any longer. That must have stressed me out so badly because, at 26 weeks, I went into labor. I was rushed to the emergency room, and in that moment, life as I knew it was about to change forever.

As I lay there in the hospital, surrounded by the sterile smell of antiseptic and the beeping of machines, I felt an overwhelming mix of fear and hope. I was about to become a mother, but the uncertainty of my situation loomed large. Would I be able to provide for my child? Would history repeat itself? The questions raced through my mind as I braced myself for the unknown.

CHAPTER 13

The Crossroads

Here we are at MUSC, and I'm just 19 years old, feeling utterly lost in the whirlwind of chaos surrounding me. I can't shake the feeling that it's too early to have this baby. It was a school day—a day that should have been filled with classes and youthful ambitions, but instead, I found myself grappling with the harsh reality of impending motherhood. Panic welled up inside of me as I wondered, "Do I call them? Who do I even call?" In that sterile hospital room, the fluorescent lights felt like they were closing in on me, amplifying my sense of dread.

Alone and scared, I dialed my church sister, Dawn. "I'm alone," I said, my voice trembling. "They say I may have to deliver my son, and he may die. I need a friend." Dawn was more than just a mentor. She was a minister I met at Abundant Life, the church that had welcomed me when I first arrived at my foster home—the same one that had cast me out for being pregnant. She was my absolute best friend, even if she was older. Dawn understood me in a way that few others did. I often joked that she had her daughter, Hedaya, "NeNe," just for me.

When Dawn arrived at the hospital, her presence felt like a lifeline. As I lay awkwardly upside down on the hospital bed, struggling to keep my son from literally sliding out, she encouraged me with soothing words. "You're not alone, Taushia. You're strong, and you can do this," she said, her voice a gentle balm to my frayed nerves. But as the minutes dragged on, fear gripped me tighter.

The medical team finally entered, their expressions serious. "We have to take him," they said, urgency lacing their voices. "If you keep him in, he won't make it, and he could also die coming out." I felt trapped, stuck between the instinct to fight for my child and the overwhelming dread that I might lose him regardless. In that moment, I had to make a decision that would haunt me: I chose to be put to sleep. If he passed, I wouldn't have to be awake to deal with the physical and emotional pain of losing him.

When I finally awoke, the world around me was a blur. As my eyes adjusted, I was met with the sight of a tiny figure being carefully cradled by a nurse. My heart raced as I processed what lay before me—a 1-pound, 8-ounce, 13-inch-long little boy with the cutest nose I had ever seen. His name was Christopher Jo'Von Delhmaine Fludd. And man, was he a fighter.

Chris faced challenges that no child should ever have to endure. He underwent over ten blood transfusions, battled septic shock, and experienced near-death moments that seemed to stretch into eternity. He was revived multiple times, sent home, and then hospitalized again, only to face death once more. Each time, he fought like a warrior, enduring seizures and the anguish of being separated from his biological mother.

As I lay in that hospital bed, a wave of despair washed over me. I was at a crossroads, grappling with the harsh reality of my situation. I was still in foster care, and the question loomed large: what foster home would take a mother and her newborn son? The thought made my chest tighten.

Just then, my caseworker walked into the room, and I braced myself for the conversation to come. "Can we go see the baby?" she asked, her tone somber yet professional. With a heavy heart, they wheeled my painfully sore body toward the neonatal unit to see Mr. Fludd. As we approached the glass enclosure, I could see the tiny figure of my son, fragile yet tenacious.

I turned to my caseworker, desperation seeping into my voice. "I don't get to be his mom?" The words hung in the air, heavy with unspoken fears and shattered dreams. The silence that followed felt suffocating. I searched her face for answers, for some glimmer of hope, but all I saw was the weight of the system that had taken so much from me.

Just when I thought I had no more tears left to cry, the realization hit me like a freight train. Would I be able to keep my son? Would I have to fight the very system that had already robbed me of so much? The questions spiraled in my mind, and I could feel the ground shifting beneath me.

As I stood on the precipice of uncertainty, I knew that the fight for my child was just beginning. The clock was ticking, and the stakes couldn't be higher. I had to navigate a world that seemed determined to keep us apart, and it felt like an insurmountable challenge.

What would I do next? How could I possibly prepare for the battles ahead? As I looked back at Christopher, his tiny fingers curling around my own, I felt the fierce determination rise within me. I would not let him go without a fight.

The doors to the neonatal unit closed behind me, and as I turned back to face my caseworker, my heart pounded with the weight of uncertainty. Would I be able to claim my role as his mother? The cliffhanger of my life hung in the balance, and the next chapter awaited.

CHAPTER 14

The Weight Of Love And Sacrifice

My son was in the fight of his life for over a year. Every day felt like a battle, and he couldn't leave the hospital until he reached at least 4 pounds. That might sound like a lot, but for a preemie, gaining just three solid pounds can take an eternity. Each day was a relentless struggle for him, and my heart felt heavy with every ounce he struggled to gain.

Christopher needed so many blood transfusions that we had to have his dad come and give blood specifically for him because the hospital was running low. It broke my heart to see him endure so much at such a tender age. He had bleeds on his brain that were causing seizures, and the doctors often spoke in hushed tones about his condition. The gravity of his situation weighed heavily on my soul.

Then, as if the universe decided to throw another obstacle in our path, Hurricane Floyd was headed for Charleston, threatening to rip us to shreds. I remember sitting in the hospital, staring out the window as the sky darkened and the winds began to howl.

"We have to evacuate," the nurse said, her tone urgent.

"I have to do what?" I asked, my voice trembling.

She repeated herself, and the reality of the situation began to sink in.

I cried out in despair, "I can't leave my son!" Just an hour before, I had been told that my son's blood was infected and that he was in septic shock. They had called in a priest, the words hanging in the air like a death sentence. He wasn't going to make it through the night, and now I was being told to leave. They handed me a number to call and sent me on my way, leaving me devastated and reeling from the news.

I explained everything to my family, who rushed to support me, and we began the arduous journey to safety. It took us 29 hours to reach Pigeon Forge, Tennessee. As we drove, I told myself I wouldn't call the hospital. I feared that if I heard the worst, I wouldn't be able to grieve him properly. But as the hours dragged on, the anxiety gnawed at me, and I finally picked up the phone.

"Miss Fludd...," the nurse's voice came through, filled with a mix of emotions. "He made it." In that instant, my heart soared and shattered simultaneously. I dropped to the ground, screaming in a mixture of joy and disbelief. People around me thought I'd lost him, but I realized what I was doing and started yelling that he made it!

The relief coursed through my veins like a healing balm, but I also knew that the next couple of months would be super hard for him. Yet, he showed me that he was a fighter, a testament to resilience and strength that I desperately needed to witness.

Back home, my situation with the Department of Social Services (DSS) hadn't magically resolved itself. They found me a home that would take me until my son was released from the hospital. But then I was left with a haunting question: what would happen next? They managed to work out a plan for me to move into an independent living apartment-style campus where mothers could live with their children. I was elated, filled with hope for the future and the prospect of starting this amazing journey with my son.

However, as the months dragged on, his progress was minimal. He wasn't being released from the hospital, and I found myself one day closer to being put out of the program meant for unwed mothers. Here I was, a mother with no baby, and the weight of that reality pressed down on me like a leaden blanket.

I fought against the mounting despair, but the inevitable happened—I lost my spot. A phone call came a week or so later from my son's grandfather. He expressed his health challenges and shared his desire to spend his last years raising his grandson. My heart sank as I realized the magnitude of the decision I had to make.

I had to remove myself from the equation, literally. Where would I go? Who would care for my son if I didn't make this choice? The questions spiraled in my mind, and I felt torn between love and sacrifice. I had to consider what was best for Christopher, and that meant making an agreement that would change the course of our lives.

It was an agonizing decision, but I knew that Christopher deserved a stable environment, especially after everything he had been through. The agreement was bittersweet. I would have to let him go into the care of his grandfather. Yet, I held onto the hope that this decision would lead to a beautiful upbringing for my son.

Over the years, a reconciliation blossomed between us, one that I'm still working on today. That little baby is now almost 26 years old, and the journey has been nothing short of miraculous. What a blessing it has been to bring pure perfection into the world.

> **Christopher,**
> **You are my inspiration, my hero, my joy,**
> **but most of all, my heart!**
> **I love you, stinka! LOL.**

As I reflect on this chapter of my life, I realize that love can be both a beautiful and painful force. The sacrifices we make for those we love can lead to unexpected paths, and while my heart ached with every decision, I know that it was all worth it in the end.

But as I look ahead, I can't help but wonder what the future holds. Would my sacrifices ultimately bring us closer together, or would they drive us further apart? The next chapter of our story awaited, filled with hope, uncertainty, and the promise of new beginnings.

CHAPTER 15

Emancipation And Awakening

So here we are... you still with me?

If you are, text me "Tacos." I'm serious! LOL!

I'm sure I'll forget I added this and wonder why y'all are doing it later! But let's get back to the journey.

As I settled into multiple homes over the next few months, a new opportunity arose. I got approved for a program that would place me into my own apartment for a year. I could hardly believe it! After everything I had endured, this felt like a glimmer of hope. Soon, I would have a space of my own, but there was a catch—I was turning 21 and being emancipated! The thought of having my independence was both exhilarating and terrifying.

You might be wondering, "Nowa, did you finish high school?" Unfortunately, that full ride I received to Meredith College to study classical voice was now just a dream in the wind. Life had taken so many unexpected turns, and the plans I had carefully crafted felt like they were slipping through my fingers.

I moved into the Nunan Street Apartments, and let me tell you, it was like stepping into a whirlwind. Whew! Let Sodom and

Gomorrah come alive! I was now a woman in my own place, with my own rules, feeling finer than wine and hotter than the Sahara. I was ready to embrace this new chapter of my life. I was getting it in, turning heads and breaking hearts, playing around like I had all the time in the world.

But as I settled into this newfound freedom, I was supposed to be learning how to live independently. I was going to have to do so eventually, yet here I was, caught up in the excitement of it all. During high school, I had met this beautiful living chocolate Barbie doll named Chamere. We hadn't become close yet, but she had introduced me to her boyfriend—now husband—back then. As fate would have it, while I was at church one day, I looked up to see the guy I'd met years ago—her now-husband—playing the keyboard at my church.

Curiosity piqued, I walked up to him and reintroduced myself. "Do you remember me?" I asked, my heart racing. He did remember my face, even if he couldn't recall my name. "Nowa," I said, and he responded, "Michael."

It was great to see him again, and I quickly learned that my current situation was Mike's friend. Excitement bubbled within me. I didn't have friends like that, and I wanted to start rolling with guys since females and I never seemed to get along. Just as I'd suspected, I was welcomed into the fold with open arms, and it felt good to be part of a group.

But man, did Mike wake me up! I'm laughing as I type this because I remember that day like it was yesterday.

"Nowa," he said, "you have to keep your hair fixed, always get dressed even if you're not going anywhere, but you can't keep coming behind me 'buss up.'"

At first, I was so mad! Who was he to tell me how to present myself? But deep down, I heard him. Someone had taken the time to guide me, to offer me constructive criticism.

For the past 26 years, he's still been helping me improve in various aspects of my life. I appreciate Michael Antonio Brown Sr. for the lessons he taught me that day and for believing in my potential when I struggled to see it myself. His friendship became a cornerstone in my life, a reminder that sometimes, you need someone to hold up a mirror and help you see what you're truly capable of.

As I navigated this new life, I found myself reflecting on the journey that had brought me to this point. The struggles, the heartbreaks, the moments of sheer despair—all of them had shaped who I was becoming. With the support of new friends like Mike, I began to believe that I could carve out a future for myself and my son, filled with hope and possibility.

But as I settled into my new routine, I couldn't shake the nagging feeling that life still had more challenges in store for me. What awaited in the next chapter of this unpredictable journey? The roads ahead were uncharted, but I was ready to face whatever lay ahead with resilience and determination.

CHAPTER 16
Emancipation And Unexpected Twists

Well, we've successfully arrived at emancipation day! I received a check for $500 and a heartfelt "Take care." It felt like a small victory, a step towards independence, and a chance to finally take control of my life. Over the next few years, I bounced around from one friend's house to another, seeking stability and a sense of belonging. Eventually, I asked Mike if I could move in with him, and to my delight, he said yes.

I nestled right onto his comfy couch, and that became my home for the next five years or so. I was ecstatic to be living with my closest friend at the time. We had the time of our lives at 4216, filled with laughter, late-night talks, and dreams for the future. I often joked about writing a collaborative book with all the members of our little club. It would surely be a wild ride filled with unforgettable stories. But life wasn't exactly a crystal stair for me, as I had once thought.

One day, I received a call from a family member saying that a sheriff was at her house looking for me. I was floored. She had no clue as to why, and panic surged through me. I decided to call the number they left, my heart racing as I did. "Come talk to us," they said. I couldn't shake the feeling that something was very wrong.

When I arrived at the sheriff's office, I could hardly believe what was happening. They arrested and booked me. I stood there in shock, grappling with the reality of my situation. You see, on Nunan Street, I had been writing checks without balancing my checkbook, resulting in seven bounced checks. I could almost hear the collective gasp. This was my first arrest.

Standing before the judge felt surreal. I was released, but not without the burden of having to pay $255 for each bounced check. You do the math. It added up quickly. I was relieved that I didn't have to go to jail, but the reality of my actions weighed heavy on my heart.

Once I returned to regular life, I focused on what truly mattered: going to church, making friends, and enjoying the little things. Mike had formed a singing group called FOCUS, and I helped them during performances by providing water, towels, and whatever else they needed. It was a joy to be part of something creative and uplifting.

One day, during a rehearsal, Mike introduced a new pianist to the group—a guy I absolutely abhorred. I couldn't believe Mike would ask him to be a part of this group. I had formed an opinion that he was self-absorbed, and I found it hard to reconcile that with my friendship with Mike.

One night, after rehearsal, Mike asked this "Mr. Self-Absorbed" to take me home, and I was fuming. I sat so close to the car door that I could've fallen out. The whole ride home was tense. I felt like a volcano ready to erupt. I thanked him as I hopped out of the car, eager to escape the awkwardness.

But just as I walked up to my door and looked back to check if he was backing out, I was met with a light shove into the door and a passionate kiss from the man I couldn't stand! What just happened? My mind raced, and I felt that concrete wall I had built around my heart crumble in an instant.

I pulled away, breathless, and asked him, "Are you sure you meant to do that?" He pulled me in close and did it again. Aww shucks! I had a boyfriend...well, kind of. I felt like I was in a romantic comedy, and I couldn't help but smile. He walked me inside, and as soon as I closed the door, I felt like a teenage schoolgirl all over again. What was this feeling?

He texted me as soon as I sat down, and we conversed for the rest of the night, my heart racing with each message. I woke up the next morning, feeling giddy, and sent him the cutest voicemail I could muster. But when he called me back, I was met with the rudest response. I sat there stunned, my heart sinking as confusion washed over me.

"Did he really just say that?" I thought, replaying the call in my mind. Each word felt like a dagger, and I couldn't understand what had just happened. I had poured my heart into that voicemail, and what did I get in return?

As I sat there, my mind racing with questions, I felt a whirlwind of emotions. Was this a sign that I should keep my guard up? Or was it just a misunderstanding? I couldn't shake the feeling that this was just the beginning of a complicated relationship. The anticipation of what was to come sent shivers down my spine.

Suddenly, my phone buzzed again, and I glanced down to see a message from an unknown number. My heart raced as I opened it, and the words made my stomach drop: "We need to talk. It's important."

What could this possibly mean? Was it about my past? About Christopher? Or something entirely different? The uncertainty hung in the air like a thick fog, and I felt a mix of dread and curiosity.

As I prepared to respond, I knew one thing for sure: life was about to take another unexpected turn, and I was bracing myself for whatever came next.

CHAPTER 17
Chaos, Courage, And New Beginnings

The voice I heard on the other end was a female, and I was stunned. "You're his girlfriend? Really?" I could hardly process her words. My heart raced as the realization hit me like a ton of bricks. All those late-night messages, the secretive phone calls—how could I have been so oblivious? I couldn't believe it. I had no clue. After a brief, tense conversation, we hung up, and my mind was a whirlwind of emotions.

I immediately called him, my anger bubbling to the surface. I cursed him out so badly that I could almost feel the heat radiating through the phone. He must have sensed the storm brewing because within moments, he pulled up outside my apartment. I stormed outside, grabbing an old butcher knife from the kitchen, fueled by a mix of betrayal and adrenaline. Before I could even reach the car, he hopped back inside in the nick of time, his eyes wide with fear.

"Miss Celie, don't do it!" My spiritual sister Meach yelled out, breaking through the haze of anger that clouded my judgment. She grabbed my hand, grounding me in that moment. I watched as he drove off, leaving me fuming in the street. That was the end of his cheating behind, or so I thought.

"Nuh uh, I'm lying," I chuckled bitterly. He stuck around for a long time, long enough to weave a dramatic tale that would eventually add "domestic violence survivor" to my grand resume of life. It was a tumultuous time filled with ups and downs, and while I was heartbroken and angry, I was also learning to stand up for myself.

But it wasn't all bad. In the midst of the chaos, I got a sweet treat out of the situation: a little 10-pound butterball turkey named RyLeigh Addisen.

Yep, we're going to go into it because, babyyyy, she's a miracle, you hear me?

The moment I found out I was pregnant with RyLeigh, the world around me shifted. Despite the turmoil in my relationship, I felt a flicker of hope igniting within me. I knew that this little girl was destined for greatness, and I was determined to give her the world. My pregnancy was filled with challenges, but each hiccup only strengthened my resolve to be the best mother I could be.

As my belly grew, so did my love for this tiny being. I attended prenatal classes, read every parenting book I could get my hands on, and surrounded myself with a network of supportive friends, like Meach. She became my rock, always reminding me that I was capable of overcoming any obstacle life threw my way.

But the road to motherhood wasn't without its bumps. I faced judgment from those who didn't understand my situation, whispers of doubt, and the lingering shadow of my past relationship. Yet, I refused to let negativity define my journey. I held my head high, determined to create a loving environment for RyLeigh.

When the day finally arrived for me to welcome my baby girl into the world, I was a bundle of nerves and excitement. I was ready to meet the miracle I had been waiting for. As I lay in the hospital bed, the pain of labor washed over me, but it was quickly overshadowed by the anticipation of holding my daughter for the first time.

After what felt like an eternity, that moment came. They placed RyLeigh in my arms, and the world around me faded away. She was a perfect 10 pounds of pure joy, and in that instant, I understood the true meaning of unconditional love. The struggles I had faced began to fade into the background as I gazed at her beautiful face with her tiny fingers wrapping around mine.

"Welcome to the world, my little butterball," I whispered, tears streaming down my cheeks. In that moment, I felt like I could conquer anything. RyLeigh was my beacon, my reason to fight, and I vowed to protect her fiercely.

As the weeks turned into months, the bond between us grew stronger. I marveled at her milestones—her first smile, her first laugh, and the way she lit up my world with each coo and giggle. I knew that we were in this together, and I was determined to give her a life filled with love, laughter, and joy.

But just when I thought I had my life back on track, the past came knocking at my door once again. Old wounds reopened, and the memories of my tumultuous relationship began to haunt me. The fear of repeating my mistakes loomed large, and I found myself grappling with insecurities I thought I had left behind.

One evening, as I rocked RyLeigh to sleep, my phone buzzed with a familiar number. My heart raced as I hesitated to answer. Could it be him? Was he back to disrupt the peace I had fought so hard to create? I glanced down at my sleeping daughter, her tiny chest rising and falling, and knew I had to confront whatever was waiting for me on the other end of that line.

Taking a deep breath, I answered the call, preparing myself for whatever storm might come. The voice on the other end sent shivers down my spine, and I braced myself for the unexpected revelations that awaited me.

"Nowa, we need to talk," the voice said, sending a chill of uncertainty through me.

What could this possibly mean? Would it be about my past, my daughter, or something entirely different? The suspense hung in the air, and I felt the weight of my choices crashing down on me as I prepared to face whatever was lying in wait.

CHAPTER 18

A Village Of Miracles

So, as I was dating before getting pregnant with RyLeigh, I faced some significant female health issues. After many surgeries, my doctor came to the resolution that children were no longer in my future. My tubes were clogged on one side and twisted on the other. It felt like a cruel twist of fate, and I was left grappling with the reality that motherhood might never be part of my story. What would any other respectable young lady do in this situation? That's right—shoot it up! Just kidding!

One night, I attended a revival service, a place where hope seemed to linger in the air like a sweet perfume. A prophet prayed for me, hands laid gently on my stomach, and I felt the warmth of healing wash over me. He declared that I was healed, and while I wanted to believe it, skepticism crept in. How could I trust such a bold statement when my reality had been so stark?

Then came the moment that changed everything: the pregnancy test. It sure made me a believer. I took five tests, just to be sure, and each one confirmed the miracle I had long thought impossible. I remember calling Chamere, my heart racing. I felt like I might vomit from the sheer shock. "I'm 30 years old and pregnant!" I told her, my voice a mix of excitement and disbelief.

In the midst of this whirlwind, I leaned on my amazing friend Addie, whom I had met at one of those concerts I told you about years earlier. I knew she would help me navigate this new chapter of my life. Addie was a rock, introducing me to an old middle school friend named Shakiya. We reconciled, and it felt like fate was guiding me toward my tribe. I was not alone during this pregnancy. Another friend, Laura, whom I'd met at those concerts, was also pregnant with RyLeigh's future best friend, Alana.

With their support, I moved into my own apartment, and together we formed a little community, ensuring that RyLeigh Addisen would make her grand entrance into the world safely. Life was about to get interesting, to say the least. I felt honored to have this opportunity again, but I was also proud and scared all at the same time.

Throughout my pregnancy, I battled a weird, irrational fear that my baby wouldn't enter this world alive. It cast a shadow over the joyous milestones, making it difficult to fully embrace the experience. Yet, I pressed on. I couldn't give up now, right? This was my chance to become a mother, and I was determined to make it count.

The day I had her wasn't even my due date—RyLeigh surprised everyone by arriving three weeks early, already weighing in at 10 pounds! Can you imagine? She was a little miracle in every sense.

When I joined Abundant Life as a teenager, there was a bratty little girl named Chelsea Nona, who clung to me like I was her mom. Every time I walked into church, she'd come running to me, her voice ringing out, "Miss Nowa!" It was always the cutest thing, and I cherished that bond we formed.

On the day I welcomed my daughter into the world, Chelsea, one of my best friends, received the call to share that moment with me. She had been there since childhood, through my pregnancy, and now she was my children's auntie, just as I was to her kiddos. The joy of having her there was immeasurable, and when she arrived at the hospital, she couldn't contain her excitement.

"Ry really is a 'whopper'!" she exclaimed, her eyes wide with delight. It was a beautiful day to be alive, filled with laughter, tears of joy, and the precious gift of motherhood. God had graced me with something unlike any other—an opportunity to love and nurture a life that was part of me.

As I held my daughter in my arms, surrounded by the love and support of the women in my life, I realized that we were about to embark on an incredible journey together. It takes a village, and I was blessed to have mine right by my side. Each woman brought her unique strength and wisdom, ready to guide me through the beautiful, chaotic, and sometimes overwhelming world of motherhood.

But just as I began to feel secure in this newfound reality, I couldn't shake the feeling that challenges were lurking just around the corner. Would I be able to navigate the complexities of parenthood? What surprises awaited me as I stepped into this new role? The excitement and trepidation swirled within me as I prepared for whatever lay ahead.

As I looked down at my beautiful daughter, the weight of responsibility settled on my shoulders. I was ready to embrace the journey, but I knew that the road ahead would require every ounce of strength and love I had.

Little did I know, the adventures of motherhood were just beginning, and life had a way of throwing unexpected twists my way.

CHAPTER 19
Trials, Triumphs, And Unseen Battles

So here I was, wondering what this man wanted to talk about while I desperately needed a break to take a shower. RyLeigh was a handful, and I was in the thick of it, balancing the demands of motherhood with the uncertainty of my past. When he finally came by, I braced myself for the conversation, but, y'all, I'm not trying to get litigated on this, okay? LOL!

It started with a request for a blood test—the kind that was supposed to offer a 99% confirmation on something that felt weighty and complicated. Then came conversations about compensation between possible parties involved. I remember the tension in the air; no plausible agreement was made, and soon enough, legal recourse was on the table, only to be removed again. More violence erupted in the aftermath, leading to no contact. And just like that, I thought, "The end!" But hold up, I'm kidding—it's definitely not the end of my story.

The years raising RyLeigh were incredibly hard. I never knew how to budget, clean properly, or be a mom. Remember, I didn't raise my son Christopher. Where was the manual? Why didn't someone write a book that applied to ALL babies? There should be a universal guide! For example, what do you mean she has a nut allergy?

OMG, I was thrown into the deep end when I got the call, "She just fell off the bed!" My heart raced, and when it happened the second time, I was a pro—at least I thought I was!

I remember her first steps, her first word, which was "aap," meaning "stop." Such simple milestones felt monumental to me, especially because I had missed so much with Chris. With RyLeigh, I savored every moment, every giggle, and every tiny victory. I didn't get it all right—Lord knows I still don't—but she's 13 now, alive, and thriving well. So kudos to me, mom and dad, and all those who have contributed to Ry's success. It definitely hasn't, and will never, go unnoticed. Hats off to you all!

Oh, and I didn't mention that somewhere in all this chaos, I ended up getting a high school diploma. I'm sprinkling this in because you haven't seen anything about a job to support this kid. It's not nationally accredited, but it was enough for me to be employed. And guess what? I've been with an amazing employer for 14 years. I even left for a year and went right back. LOL! Suffice it to say, I'm in love with the mobile—cue the tune of "In Love with the Coco."

But for the life of me, I couldn't understand why, after having my daughter, I struggled to succeed. Though I still didn't know how to budget, I would come into so much money that I could blow it and still handle my bills. But this felt different. It was almost as if something was holding me back, something spiritual—dare I say, demonic.

Guess what? It was...

The realization hit me one evening as I sat on the couch, RyLeigh asleep in her room. I felt the weight of my past pressing down on me, like a dark cloud that wouldn't lift. I'd fought hard to break free from the chains that held me back, yet it felt like I was still tethered to something I couldn't see. The doubts crept in, whispering that I wasn't good enough, that I didn't deserve success.

With RyLeigh growing up, I wanted to be a beacon of light for her, a source of strength and inspiration. But how could I do that when I felt so lost? I pondered the struggles I had faced and the demons I believed I had conquered, only to find myself grappling with new ones.

In my heart, I knew I needed to confront these challenges head-on. It was time to break the cycle of fear and doubt, to step boldly into the life I envisioned for my daughter and myself. I reflected on the support system I built—the friends who rallied around me, the women who became my village. They helped me navigate the tumultuous waters of motherhood, and I needed to lean on them now more than ever.

As I sat there, an idea began to crystallize in my mind. I could turn this struggle into a source of strength. I could share my story, my journey, and hopefully inspire others who felt trapped in their circumstances. Maybe, just maybe, by shedding light on my own darkness, I could help others find their way.

With renewed determination, I resolved to seek help and find a therapist who could guide me through the shadows that had lingered too long. I knew that healing wouldn't come overnight, but I was ready to take that first step. I wanted to be the mother RyLeigh deserved, and I was willing to fight for it.

As I lay down that night, I felt a flicker of hope in my heart. I was ready to reclaim my narrative, fight for my future, and embrace the beautiful, messy journey of motherhood. With RyLeigh by my side, I knew that together, we could face whatever challenges lay ahead.

The next chapter of my life was waiting, and I was determined to step into it with courage, resilience, and a newfound sense of purpose.

CHAPTER 20
The Comedy Of Errors

So, I started this journey to healing, and here I am—mentally and emotionally bruised and battered—trying to be the best version of myself, but I just couldn't get right. Have you ever seen the movie, "Life" with Eddie Murphy? There was a character named "Can't Get Right," and I swear that's what I felt like—Can't Get Right was my middle name. Repo after repo, eviction after eviction, and depression so deep I'd forget moments in time. My mental health was deteriorating faster than my bank account.

I found myself relying on demonic voices to guide me. What happened to church? I'm glad you asked! I was still a faithful member—didn't say I was possessed, LOL! But I was absolutely listening to a voice that was praying for my demise, and I had no clue. It's like I signed up for the wrong spiritual membership!

I started getting diagnosed and placed on different medications for anxiety and insomnia, and it was all just so crazy and confusing. It felt like a reality show where the producers were throwing curveballs at me left and right. When I sat down with all my troubles, it was like something wasn't adding up.

Let me give you a little more insight.

I'm a dreamer. I always have been. If I wasn't dreaming, I knew I wasn't in a good place with God. I hadn't dreamt anything significant in quite some time, but one particular night, I had a dream that took me straight to my grandfather's house. Now, my granddaddy's name was Louis "KingDog" Fludd, and I loved him dearly. His house, when I was a little girl, looked like a gray rickety shack. You had to step carefully on the porch boards or risk falling through—talk about a DIY hazard!

In my dream, I was inside preparing for some friends' arrival, and another acquaintance was on the porch sweeping. I thought she was helping me clean up, but then I heard her laughing and talking to multiple people who hadn't even arrived yet. It was just us, or so I thought. So, I walked to the screen door to see who she was talking to, and lo and behold, I saw what looked like fully dressed dead ancestors sitting in the rocking chairs on the porch. I mean, who invited the spooky family reunion?

She was giving them instructions on bad things to do to people. I heard her tell one of them to stick its foot out to "trip" one of our friends. Sure enough, as the friend walked up, he tripped over nothing—classic! He looked around, trying to figure out what he'd stumbled over, while she and the ancestors laughed like they were at a comedy show. I immediately said, "That's not funny!"

The acquaintance was shocked that I could see what she saw. "Yes, I see y'all!" I declared, and then I woke up. That was the day I knew something was off. Yet, I still remained connected in real life, convincing myself—or something convinced me—that God was wrong about this person. Can you believe that? I can't!

It took years for me to snap out of it, which brings us to the current day. I was so proud because here I am, free from any bondage that so easily beset me before. I thought I was ready to recover, but you didn't think that demon I served freely through sex, drugs, and lies was going to let me go that easily, did you?

Don't stress! I did too! I've been addicted to pills, liquor, and sex for the majority of my life. I found myself hypersexual from childhood trauma. I would get as high and drunk as I could and have sex with whomever I chose to. I popped painkillers to numb myself during these moments, lied to cover up infidelity, and didn't care. I was the walking definition of morally immoral. Yep, doing nasty stuff but had the nerve to set rules on my nastiness—like, "No eye contact during the sinning!"

I had hit an all-time low. I was proudly doing porn, making great strides with it too. I'd left the church and was just chillin'. Life was leveling out, or so I thought. It was like I was in a dark comedy, starring me as the lead who couldn't get her act together, and the audience was dying laughing—except nobody was laughing with me.

The struggle was real, but somewhere in the chaos, I held onto the hope that I could turn this narrative around. After all, every great comedy has a moment where the protagonist finally gets it together, right? I was just waiting for my punchline.

CHAPTER 21
The Journey Of Healing And Redemption

So here we are. When I say "we," I mean the many layers of my existence, each one contributing to the tapestry of who I am today. You see, I had an alter ego that helped me navigate the tumultuous waters of my life—a version of myself that allowed me to "be" someone I knew I was not. Taylor Port, that sweet elixir, got ya girl through some wild moments. During those times of temporary insanity, I was grappling with overwhelming burdens. Over ten close friends had slept with my one "boyfriend". I carried the pain of past pregnancies I aborted, faced a delivery I could never discuss, mourned the loss of a child, and endured the trauma of being raped and molested. I experienced homelessness, joblessness, suicidal thoughts, and a porn addiction—all of it crashing down on me like a relentless storm. Ya girl was bad off.

In the midst of this chaos, I left the church, and in my mind, I left God too. I was living my so-called "BEST life" outside the confines of traditional morality, indulging in sex, drugs, and spirits. But one day, I received an invitation to a church service. My old high school friends, including Ra'Shan and Donald—two of my closest male friends—were hosting a revival-like service and encouraged me to come. I declined, thinking, "I'm good." I was living in a hotel, down bad financially, but deep down, I knew I needed to attend. However, I convinced myself that making money for the week was my priority.

After making my money, I received another invitation not too long after. This time, I went. The atmosphere was electric, and it felt like home—the kind of feel that reminded me of the Pentecostal Holiness roots I came from. That night, I made a silent promise. If I could find a church that felt like this, I'd at least consider attending regularly. Little did I know, God had me on His mind all along. My high school friends had started a church called the Impact City of Charleston. Bishop Ra'Shan Lamar Wilson is my pastor, and Executive Pastor Donald is, well, my executive pastor! How wild is that, considering we were quite the wild bunch growing up?

Initially, I wasn't going to join—I'd had my fill of church experiences where the older generation made you feel ashamed for getting pregnant out of wedlock. I had to apologize to the church for my past mistakes, and I was done with that kind of judgment. So, I thought I'd attend but wouldn't join. Lies, all lies! I joined, and God took me on a remarkable 44-year journey to bring me right back to Him.

I did it! I came back to God! The excitement bubbled within me as I thought, "Let's go, God! I'm ready to serve you!" But then... BOOM! Thyroid cancer. Excuse me? Yes! I received the diagnosis, and the only solution was surgery. My heart sank. I talk for a living—I do voiceovers and sing! How could I continue with a surgery looming over me? But I had to have the surgery, so I went through with it, fully aware of the risks, convinced it wouldn't happen to me. Yet, it did. I woke up to find out I had a paralyzed vocal cord.

Immediately, I thought, "Are you serious? I come back to God, and this is what I get? Devil, you must be pretty mad, huh?" As I began to recover, just 90 days later, I found myself in church one night, feeling sluggish. I had traveled from South Carolina to Alabama and back in less than 24 hours, so I figured that was the cause of my fatigue. However, after attending a funeral and struggling to settle in, I decided to head to the emergency room.

What I heard next shocked me to my core: "You had a heart attack." Nuh uh! I literally asked the Lord if He was kidding. Y'all wouldn't believe it—I walked out of the hospital two days later, healed once again! A 98% blockage had been reduced to less than 25% when I left. You can't tell me what God can't do!

Yes, you read that right. All that I had endured led me to this moment. The person God healed is now on a journey to becoming the healer. How could I help anyone if I hadn't gone through the fire myself? I went through for you! Want me to prove it? You're still reading! I made it! I'm making it! And so are you! What's your story? Why haven't you told it? This is your sign—just start writing.

I still hear Bishop Ra'Shan's voice echoing in my mind, urging, "Just start writing." That's what I did. Do it! Trust me! A lot of my story has been condensed to protect some, but much of it is not. I'm honored that you thought enough to invest your hard-earned money to purchase my life on a page.

As I close this chapter, I prophesy that the pen you use to write your story will be the same pen you use to sign your checks. Your words carry weight. They have the power to transform lives, including your own.

So, I'll see you in the next book. I'm excited for the journey that lies ahead—not just for me but for you as well. Together, let's embrace the healing, the struggles, and the victories that come with sharing our stories.

Remember, you are not alone in this journey. Your voice matters, and it's time to let it be heard.

Remember, we're on a JOURNEY to healing!

Nowa

ABOUT THE AUTHOR

NOWA ARKTRESHIA

A Story of Strength, Survival, and Purpose

Born and raised in Snowden, a rural unincorporated community in Mount Pleasant, SC, Nowa Arktreshia grew up in a world that felt anything but secure. Her childhood was strange—happiness was not something she remembers holding onto. Instead, it was shaped by experiences no child should have to endure. Being touched inappropriately at a young age left deep wounds, ones that dictated much of who she was. But they did not define who she would become. God did.

Her time in foster care was complex, a mix of pain and unexpected joy. While instability was a constant, there were also moments of adventure—skiing, white water rafting, kayaking, and camping in different states. These experiences were a rare light in a system that too often dims the spirits of those within it.

As a teen mother, she faced one of the hardest decisions of her life: to give her son up or to keep him with her, knowing the struggles he would have to endure by her side. The weight of that decision never left her, and every choice she made was with him in mind. But it was when her daughter came along that she had a painful realization—her children were watching her and learning from her. Every decision and every mistake, had the power to shape their futures. That was the wake-up call. If she didn't change, the cycle would continue. And that was not an option.

Faith became her foundation. Not just in theory, but in survival. God was the only reason she was still here. The book of Romans was her anchor, a place she turned to when life became unbearable. And the story of Rahab reminded her that redemption was always possible, no matter what the past held.

Though she has yet to begin school, her path is clear. With plans to pursue PreMed and a minor in Criminal Justice, she is determined to become a Crime Scene

Investigator. Curiosity is in her nature— she's nosy and unashamed of it. Her mind doesn't settle for easy answers. It dissects problems from every angle. She doesn't just want to observe—she wants to solve.

Her debut book, ***The Crown And The Scars***, was born from heartbreak. Writing was not just a creative outlet. It was a necessity. It became her way of reclaiming her story, of transforming pain into power. Through these pages, she isn't just sharing her truth—she is giving others the courage to do the same. She hopes readers will walk away not only understanding her better but also realizing they have the strength to tell their own stories.

If there is one lesson life has taught Nowa Arktreshia, it's this: The only person who is sure for you—is you. But that doesn't mean she walks alone. She moves forward, carrying her faith, her resilience, and the unwavering belief that she was meant for more. And she is just getting started!

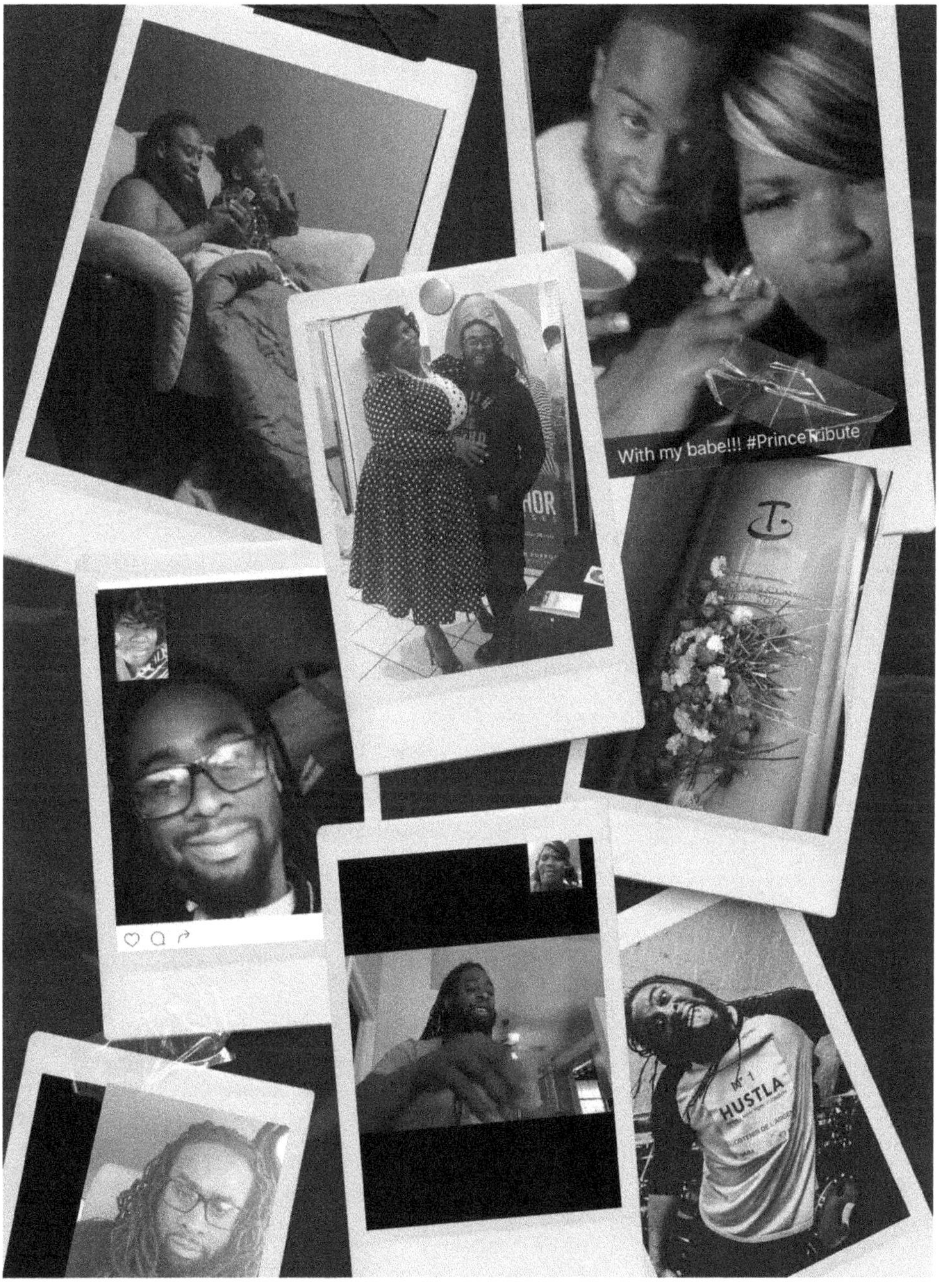
With my babe!!! #PrinceTribute
HUSTLA

www.ingramcontent.com/pod-product-compliance
Lightning Source LLC
LaVergne TN
LVHW061040070526
838201LV00073B/5115